T0025540

THE BACKYARD BUG

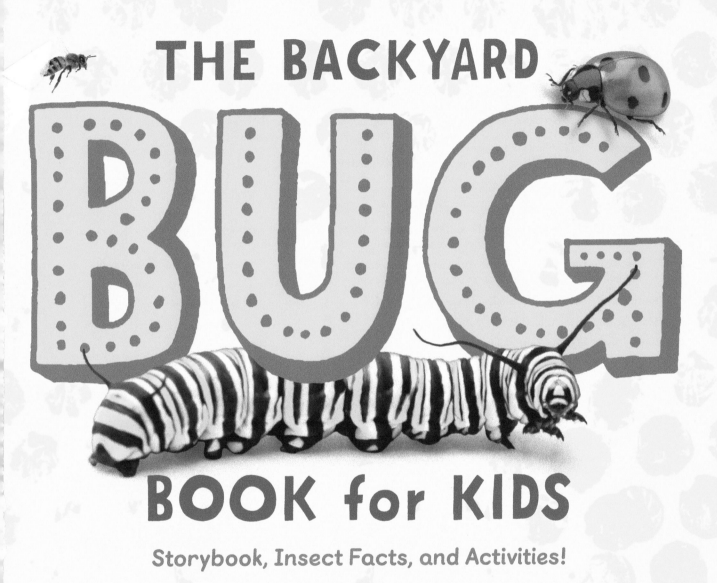

BOOK for KIDS

Storybook, Insect Facts, and Activities!

Lauren Davidson

ROCKRIDGE
PRESS

Copyright © 2019 by Rockridge Press

All rights reserved. No part of this publication may be reproduced, stored in a retrieval system, or transmitted in any form or by any means, electronic, mechanical, photocopying, recording, scanning, or otherwise without the prior written permission of the Publisher. Requests to the Publisher for permission should be addressed to the Permissions Department, Rockridge Press, 1955 Broadway, Suite 400, Oakland, CA 94612.

First Rockridge Press hardcover edition 2022

Originally published in trade paperback by Rockridge Press 2019

Rockridge Press and the Rockridge Press logo are trademarks or registered trademarks of Callisto Media Inc. and/or its affiliates in the United States and other countries and may not be used without written permission.

For general information on our other products and services, please contact our Customer Care Department within the United States at (866) 744-2665, or outside the United States at (510) 253-0500.

Hardcover ISBN: 979-8-88608-532-7 | Paperback ISBN: 978-1-64152-525-1 | eBook ISBN: 978-1-64152-526-8

Manufactured in the United States of America

Interior and Cover Designer: Stephanie Sumulong
Art Producer: Sue Bischofberger
Editor: Jeanine Le Ny
Production Editor: Andrew Yackira

Photography: Alex Staroseltsev/shutterstock, cover; Cameramannz/shutterstock, cover, pp. 4, 8, 18, 31, 36-37, 42; Antagain/iStock, cover, p. 35; Sari ONeal/shutterstock, p. 3; AttaBoyLuther/iStock, p. 5; Cameramannz/shutterstock, pp. 6, 14, 26, 32; InsectWorld/shutterstock, p. 7; Dmytro Khlystun/shutterstock, p. 9; Jacob Hamblin/shutterstock, pp. 10, 20; Mark Brandon/shutterstock, pp. 11, 39, 41; brackish_nz/shutterstock, pp. 12, 16, 22, 24, 28; Peter Yeeles/shutterstock, p. 13; Irochka_T/iStock, p. 15; frank60/shutterstock, p. 17; DeSid/iStock, p. 19; KeithSzafranski/iStock, p. 21; Mauro Rodrigues/shutterstock, p. 23; tomark/iStock, p. 25; Fer Gregory/shutterstock, p. 27; stanley45/iStock, pp. 29, 40; Liliboas/iStock, pp. 30, 40; AmbientIdeas/iStock, pp. 33, 36-37, 39, 42, 46; Vonkara1/iStock, pp. 34-35, 39, 42, 46; Cristina Romero Palma/shutterstock, pp. 34-35, 39, 44, 46; Valengilda/iStock, pp. 34, 36-38, 45-46; GlobalP/iStock, pp. 34, 36-37, 39, 45; Cosmin Manci/shutterstock, pp. 35, 41; DanielaAgius/iStock, pp. 35, 46; eli_asenova/iStock, pp. 36-37, 41; Kaphoto/iStock, pp. 36-37, 45-46; irin-k/shutterstock, pp. 39, 46; Binh Thanh Bui/shutterstock, p. 39; Jay Ondreicka/shutterstock, p. 40; xu3l54tj06/shutterstock, p. 40; Anton Kozyrev/shutterstock, p. 41; fotomak/shutterstock, p. 43; Yosuke Hasegawa/shutterstock, pp. 44-45; Subbotina Anna/shutterstock, p. 46.

Photograph of the author courtesy of Mackenzie Goodman

10 9 8 7 6 5 4 3 2 1 0

I'm coming out to meet the world,
from my safe and cozy pearl.

Fact:
A caterpillar larva
hatches by chewing
out of its tiny eggshell.
Then it eats the rest
as a snack.

3

A tiny, hungry caterpillar,
I'll give this leaf a whirl.

Fact:
Caterpillars can grow to be 1,000 times their original size. They shed their skins as they get bigger and bigger.

I munch and munch and eat all day
and wonder what to do.

I ask a spotted ladybug,
"Will I grow to look like you?"

Fact:
Adult ladybugs have two sets of wings. The hard wings on the outside protect soft flying wings underneath.

I see a giant grasshopper.
He's jumping very high.

I hope to hop like him one day,
and maybe touch the sky.

8

Fact:
If grasshoppers were human sized, they could cross the length of an entire football field in one giant leap!

Wow! That bug is beautiful—
so colorful and bright.

Could I ever have such pretty wings?
Perhaps one day I might.

Fact:
There are close to
15,000 kinds of jewel
beetles around the world.
They come in lots of
different colors.

There's a cricket in the bushes
making noise by rubbing wings.

I wonder who he's singing to
with all the joy he brings.

12

Fact:
Only male crickets can sing. All crickets have tiny ears on their front legs.

What is all that buzzing
so high up in the trees?
They're making a big hive up there.
That's a home for bees!

Fact:
Honeybees tell each other where to find the best pollen and nectar by doing the waggle dance.

Look at all those tiny ants—
so little, yet so tough.

Maybe I'll be strong like them
one day when I'm grown up.

16

Fact:
Some ants can pick up objects that are fifty times their own body weight. That would be like a person lifting a rhinoceros!

That sticky web this spider spins
is dangerous, I know.

I have a hunch, I'll be her lunch
if I don't turn and go!

18

Fact:
Spiders are not insects—they are arachnids. Most spiders feed on bugs and insects, but some can catch and eat frogs, lizards, and even birds.

Hey, did that brown stick just move?
Can it really be?

Oh, it's not a stick at all.
That sneaky bug just tricked me!

20

Fact:
Stick insects can hide really well. This protects them from birds and other animals that might eat them.

Oops! I scared a roly poly.
It's hiding and so small,

with head and body nice and snug,
and rolled up in a ball.

Fact:
Guess what—roly polies are not insects. They are crustaceans, just like lobsters.

That lovely insect darts and glides
way up in the air.
I wish one day to fly as high
without a single care.

24

Fact:
Dragonflies are superfast and expert hunters. They can even fly backward.

Floating and glowing in the early night sky
are special beetles called fireflies.
I wonder as I grow and grow
if one day I will brightly glow.

Fact:
Fireflies use their flashy lights to attract mates or even prey!

I'm so big. It's time to sleep
right here on this tree.
I'll make a home, cozy up alone,
and dream of what I'll be.

28

Fact:
A caterpillar's body forms into a little house called a chrysalis. Inside the house, the caterpillar's body changes again.
Can you guess what happens next?

One . . .   two . . .   three . . .

This is me!

Fact:
A caterpillar turns into
a beautiful butterfly.

BUGGY BONUS
GAMES & ACTIVITIES

Cute Caterpillar

Trace the caterpillar.

Beautiful Butterfly

Trace the butterfly.

Make a Match

Draw a line to match each picture to its shadow.

34

Show What You Know

Put an X on the ones that are **not** insects.

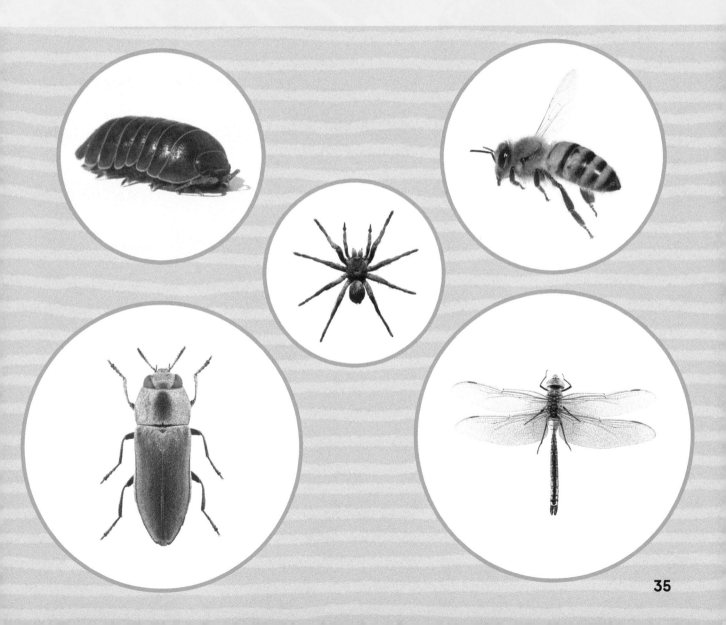

Who's Next?

Can you finish the patterns? Circle each answer.

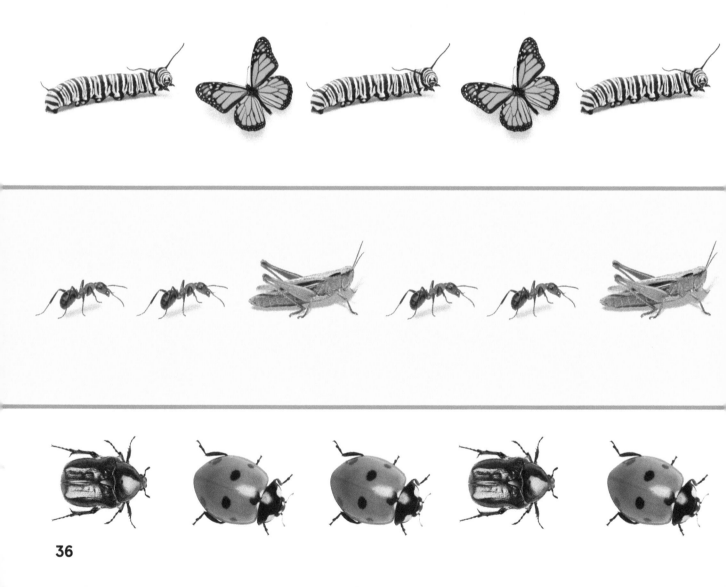

Seeing Spots

Count the spots on each ladybug.

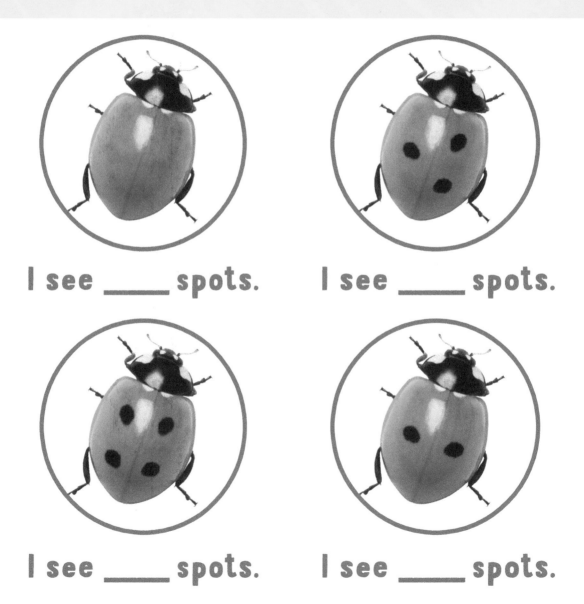

I see _____ spots.   I see _____ spots.

I see _____ spots.   I see _____ spots.

Honeybees!

Follow the honeybees to the flower.
Then do the waggle dance!

Butterfly Life Cycle

Draw a line to match each picture to a word.

eggs

caterpillar

chrysalis

butterfly

Beetle Party

Get the jewel beetle to its friends. Draw a path.

Munch, Munch!
Which path leads to the yummy leaf?

1   2   3

Special Spider

Draw a path to the center of the web.

Peek-a-Bug!

There are 5 bugs and insects hidden in the picture.
Can you find them all?

Friends with Wings

Find and circle the ones with wings before they fly away!

About the Author

Lauren Davidson is a practicing entomologist, but she prefers the term "bug mom." Her daily life involves unpacking shipments of butterflies, cleaning up after cockroaches, and educating kids about "buggy" things. Visit her online at Bugsologist.com.

Answer Key

Make a Match
Draw a line to match each picture to its shadow.

Show What You Know
Put an X on the ones that are not insects.

Who's Next?
Can you finish the patterns? Circle each answer.

Seeing Spots
Count the spots on each ladybug.

I see _0_ spots.   I see _3_ spots.

I see _4_ spots.   I see _2_ spots.

Honeybees!
Follow the honeybees to the flower.
Then do the waggle dance!

Butterfly Life Cycle
Draw a line to match each picture to a word.

eggs

caterpillar

chrysalis

butterfly

Beetle Party
Get the jewel beetle to its friends. Draw a path.

Munch, Munch!
Which path leads to the yummy leaf?

1   2   3

Special Spider
Draw a path to the center of the web.

Peek-a-Bug!
There are 5 bugs and insects hidden in the picture.
Can you find them all?

Friends with Wings
Find and circle the ones with wings before they fly away!

Printed in the USA
CPSIA information can be obtained
at www.ICGtesting.com
CBHW050921300524
9268CB00002B/5